Let's Take Care of Our New Budgerigar

Alejandro Algarra / Rosa M. Curto

BARRON'S

A fantastic birthday present

Alice is a very curious girl and a great animal lover.
For her eighth birthday, she has asked for a budgerigar
as a present, like the one she saw in her friend's house.
She can't wait for the great day, and she enjoys imagining
what her new talkative friend will be like.

First the house

Her birthday has arrived and Peter, Alice's little brother, leads his sister by the hand to the living room. "Don't open your eyes yet!" says Peter. When they reach the living room and Alice opens her eyes, she sees a large birdcage on the table. "First we have to prepare their house," says Mom. "We'll soon be able to collect its new residents." "Residents?" asked Alice. "Yes, in the pet shop, they advised us to buy a couple of budgerigars, so they won't get lonely." "Yippee!" shouts Alice and Peter.

Things about the cage

Alice and Peter amuse themselves preparing the things the cage needs to have:

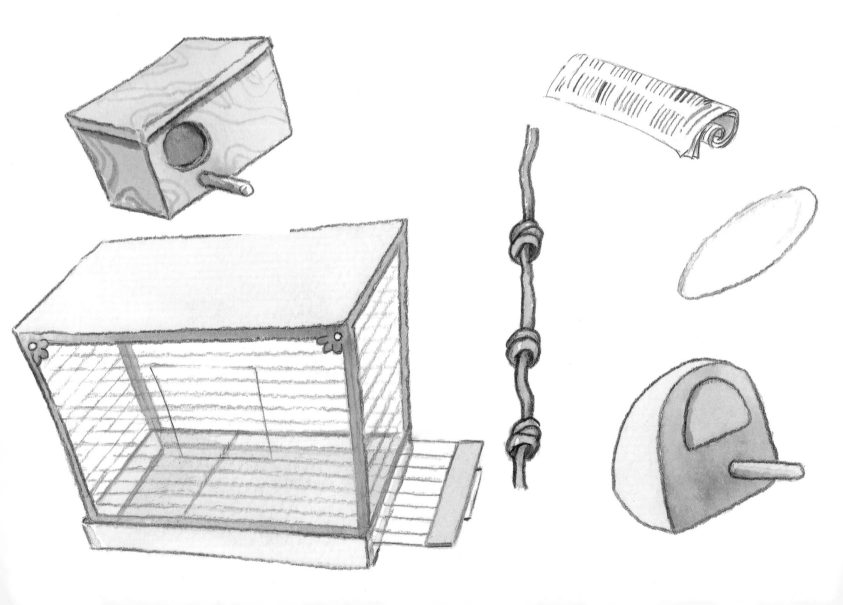

- The cage is quite large. It's made of metal with horizontal bars. There's enough room for a pair of budgerigars. It has two doors.
- The floor has a metal grill, which separates the budgerigars from their excrement and food remains that may have fallen down. A removable tray allows the paper underneath to be changed as needed.
- There's a feeder for each bird hung on the inside of the cage. A couple of little bowls could also be used.
- Tube-shaped drinking troughs prevent the water from getting dirty.
- Perches: Two unvarnished wooden bars are placed side by side in the cage at different heights, far enough apart for the birds to fly from one to the other.
- Toys.

Let's go to the pet shop!

Alice and Peter's family always goes to a trustworthy pet shop, where they know the animals are well looked after and they can rely on the shop assistants' advice.

At last, Alice is in front of the cage where the budgerigars are waiting to meet their new owners. Alice asks Peter to help her choose one. "You must look for attentive and clean budgerigars that have well preened plumage." "Look at this one," says Peter, "do you like it?" "Yes!" replies Alice. "And I would like that other one over there, on the perch above yours."

What are the budgerigars like?

The budgerigar that Peter chose is very pretty. It has blue feathers on its belly and chest, black, white, and some blue feathers on the wings and head, and a white face. In the shop, the children were told that it was a male. It's called Charlie. The one Alice chose is different. It has a green chest and belly, the wings have touches of black and yellow, and the head has black stripes on an almost totally yellow head. It also has a little blue mark on each side of its head. It's a lovely female, and its name is Polly.

The first few days

Charlie and Polly spent their first few days in the cage, which was prepared for the couple a few days before they arrived. The cage is positioned in a well-lit place, away from the kitchen, drafts of air, and appliances such as the television or stereo. Naturally, the budgerigars were scared during the first few days, and when Alice carefully placed her hand in the cage to clean it and change the food, they became very nervous. They will soon forget their fears and get used to the presence and voices of all the members of the family.

Watch how they play!

Budgerigars are very intelligent birds. Each one has its own personality. They are naturally curious and enjoy playing with objects around them and biting them. Peter and Alice have placed a couple of swings in the cage that the budgerigars can climb onto and even sleep on. They love making the little bells ring that the children have hung from one of the perches. Dad helped the children to make a knotted rope hanging from the roof of the cage. Polly and Charlie climb up the rope and bite it. Every month, the children place new toys in the cage so that the budgerigars don't get bored.

The food

Alice already knows what she should always place in each feeder: a handful of mixed seeds and some nutritious pellets. The budgerigars love eating the fresh fruit and vegetables that the children place between the bars. At first, they weren't very interested, but they got used to it and now they love it. The children always wash the fruit and vegetables thoroughly before giving them to the budgerigars. They have also added a cuttlefish for them to eat, so that their bones will always be healthy.

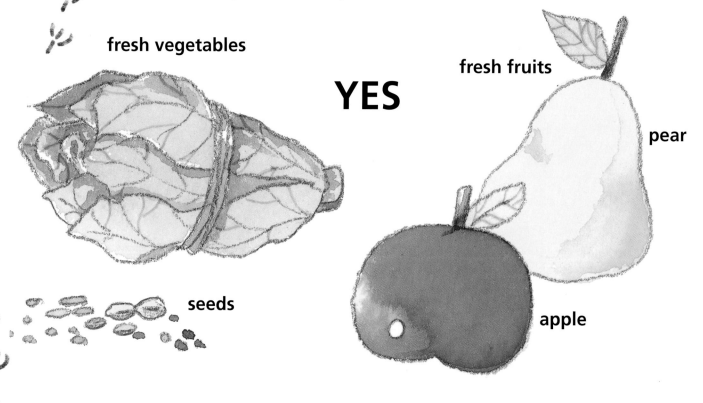

fresh vegetables

YES

fresh fruits

pear

seeds

apple

NO

citrus fruits

onions

potatoes

parsley

TOXIC

avocado

chocolate

Cleanliness is very important

Alice and Peter always keep Charlie and Polly's cage clean. They change the newspaper in the tray every week and clean the tray thoroughly. Also, after feeding, they remove any fruit and vegetable remains from the cage and bars. They clean the perches with a damp sponge whenever they are dirty.

They also wipe the bars with the sponge.
They change the drinking water daily so
it is always clean.

Two very affectionate little birds

Like all little budgerigars, Polly and Charlie enjoy living in company. It's like they couldn't live without each other. When they eat, they like to pass crushed pieces of food from beak to beak. They also help each other to keep their plumage clean. They scratch each other with their beaks, especially on the neck. When they're tranquil, they spend a lot of time being affectionate and preening each other. They often do this before falling asleep together on the perch. Alice turns off the light in the room: It's time to go to sleep!

Bath time!

Alice places a container serving as a bath inside the cage. She adds a little warm water, about one inch (2 or 3 cm). There is nothing else in the water: It's important not to use any kind of soap or perfume. Polly loves the idea. She curiously inspects the bath at once and she goes inside, opening out her plumage. It's especially good at the moment, because she's molting and she's quite itchy. On the other hand, Charlie is not so convinced and prefers not to go in. Alice has found a solution for him: She sprays him with water, like rain.

NO

perfumes

soap

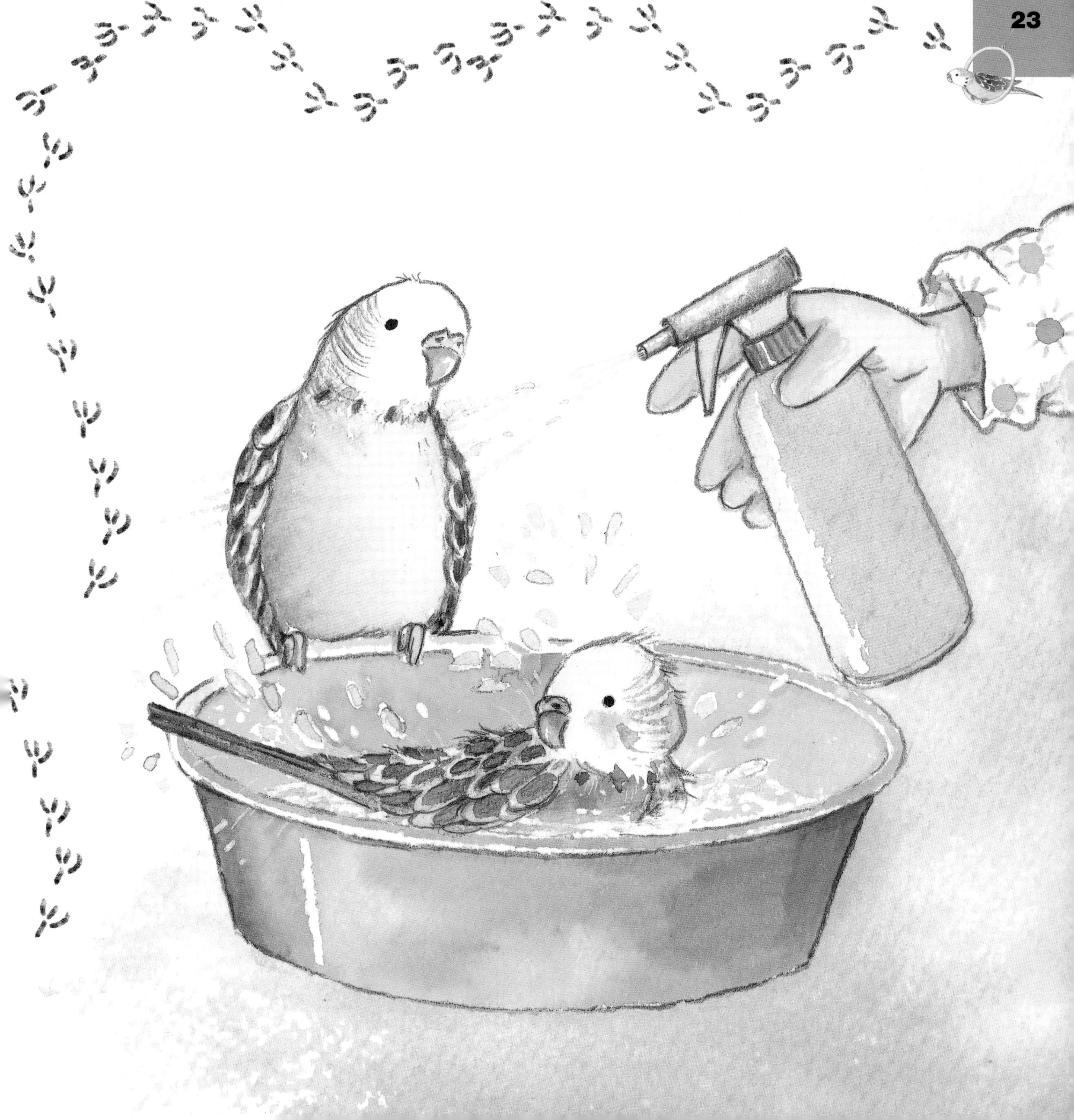

Flying!

Today, the budgerigars are going to have great fun: For the first time, they'll be allowed to fly around the room and investigate everything. First, Alice closes all the windows so they can't escape, and then she closes the curtains so they don't bang into the windows. The children open the cage doors and Charlie is the first to stick his head out and go outside. He flies around the room a couple of times and then lands on top of a piece of furniture. Polly goes out next and after flying around for a while lands on the curtain rail. How happy they are!

Good friends

Alice wants her budgerigars to trust her and climb on her hands fearlessly. Polly and Charlie have gotten used to seeing her hands enter the cage to give them food and clean it, and they're not startled. Alice offers them a piece of apple, their favorite food, with her hand inside the cage. At first, they're startled and don't dare to go close. Every day, Polly seems braver, and one day she takes the piece of apple. The next day, she climbs onto Alice's fingers to take it. Little by little, she forgets her fears and now she almost always climbs onto the hand. Charlie took longer, but he has finally learned to do it as well.

Teach them to talk

Peter loves listening to the budgerigars talking, so whenever he's with them, he repeats some words to see if they can learn them. For instance, whenever Alice brings the food, Peter says "Hello, hello!" One day, when everyone was in the dining room, Peter passed by the budgerigars' cage and he heard Charlie say something.
He went closer and heard him repeat the word *hello*. What joy! Peter understood two things: that the budgerigar could talk and that he was hungry!

The best care

Alice is pleased with her budgerigars. She's fascinated by their colors, their intelligence, and with how affectionate they are. What joy when she goes near the cage and they call out to her! They approach the bars to where they can see her, taking little steps with their claws on the perch, and they sometimes even whistle to show their affection. Peter also has a lot of fun with these pets. He loves watching how they caress each other and "give each other little kisses," as he says. Charlie and Polly are also very comfortable in their home, because the children look after them very well. They keep them clean and give them a lot of affection.

A toy for your budgerigars

It's easy to make toys for your budgerigars. You can adapt them to their tastes, and also, for a small price, you can offer them new toys often, so that they don't lose interest. Use your imagination, and above all, use materials that are not harmful to your pets. Budgerigars love nibbling everything. Let's make a toy for biting and climbing that will also be attractive to them because of its colors.

Materials

**colored beads
(they can also be made of hard plastic)**

**large wooden beads
(unpainted ones are better)**

Scissors

cardboard

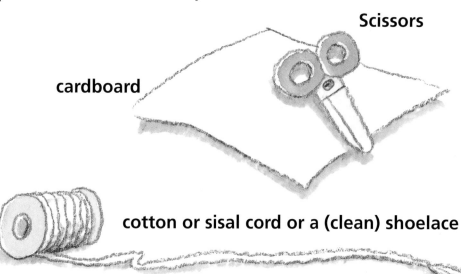

cotton or sisal cord or a (clean) shoelace

Instructions:

1. Cut out circles and squares from the cardboard, without jutted edges. Make a small hole in the middle of each piece.
2. Knot one end of the cord.
3. Thread together the colored and wooden beads and cardboard cutouts in a chain.
4. Tie a knot at the other end of the cord.

You can add little bells to the chain; the budgerigars love the sound. Never use bells with holes in them, as they can harm their claws if they get trapped in the grooves.

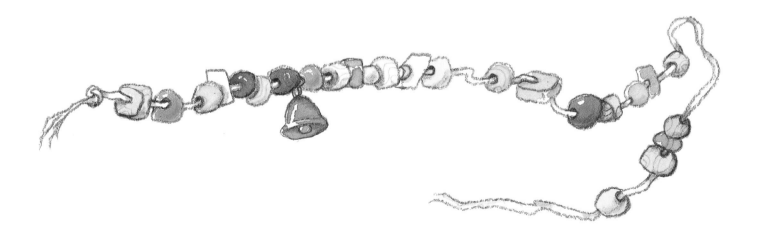

Advice from the veterinarian

HOW TO CHOOSE YOUR BUDGERIGAR

When buying a budgerigar, you should consider this advice. You should choose your budgerigar from the liveliest and cleanest birds in the cage. The bird should appear attentive and active. The plumage should be shiny and smooth, with no "un-preened" feathers sticking out. The feathers around the bird's bottom should be clean and dry, without any excrement remains. You should also check the appearance of the feet, nails, and beak. The beak should be a normal shape and have dry, clean nostrils.

BUDGERIGAR CHARACTERISTICS

Budgerigars live in large groups in their natural habitat. Furthermore, they partner for life. So, it is advisable to acquire at least two budgerigars as pets, ideally a male and a female. If you don't want them to reproduce, simply don't provide them with a nesting box. It is also possible to have a pair of males without any problems. It's more difficult to keep a pair of females, as they may fight. Several features serve to distinguish between the two sexes on adult birds, such as the color of the ceres (the lower part of the beak). It is usually blue in male birds and ranges from pink to gray-brown on females. However, among very young budgerigars, these differences are hardly noticeable. If you're not sure, you can ask for help in the shop or from a specialist to determine the sex of each member of the couple. The younger the budgerigars are, the easier it will be to train them and get them used to you. Very young budgerigars have a series of grooves on their heads. The color of their eyes is also a good indicator of age: The black color covers the whole eye in young birds. As they get older, a white ring appears, like the white part of human eyes, which grows with age.

THE CAGE

It's very important to choose a good cage, where the budgerigars will feel more comfortable and have enough space to climb and do some exercise—the bigger the better. The minimum size is 18 by 18 inches and 20 inches high (45 by 45 cm and 50 cm high). Cages with square or rectangular bases are preferable to circular ones. It should be made of a rustproof metal; wooden cages are no good, as the budgerigars can bite and break them. The distance between the bars should be from .3 to .5 inch (8 to 13 mm). Horizontal bars are better, as budgerigars love climbing. The cage should be of an acceptable quality, without burrs on the bars or parts sticking out where they could hurt themselves. With respect to the doors, those that open sideways or downward are better. The cage should have more than one door, allowing access from several points, which is useful when cleaning the cage.

CAGE FEATURES

Several features should be placed in the cage to make up the budgerigars' home. It's important for them to have several types of perches. They need at least two, preferably made of wood and placed at different levels. Ideally, they should have perches of different diameters to promote exercise and stimulate their feet muscles. An alternative advisable option is to use natural tree branches. They should be clean and free from pesticides: resinous conifer wood is unsuitable. Toys that can be placed in the cage include swings, at least one for each budgerigar, and little rustproof metal bells. They will also enjoy playing with a knotted cord, which should be thick enough to prevent them from becoming entangled in it. If the knotted cord is hung from the roof of the cage, they

will bite the rope and climb up it. Finally, the floor should have a grill and a tray underneath it covered with newspaper, which should be changed often.

FEEDING

A couple of feeders should be placed for feeding the birds; those hung inside the cage are better. Regarding drinking troughs, the best ones are tubes. None of these containers should be placed directly below the perches, as they will end up full of excrement. It is advisable to provide the birds with a varied diet. They can be fed a mixture of seeds and prepared food (pellets), complemented with a variety of fresh fruit and vegetables. You should never give them citrus fruits, parsley, potatoes, or onions. Under no circumstances should you give the birds avocado or chocolate: Both are highly toxic to them. With a varied diet, there's no need for a vitamin supplement, apart from a source of calcium. You can provide them with this by simply hanging a piece of cuttlefish inside the cage.

TRAINING AND BEHAVIOR

The budgerigar is one of the birds that best learns to imitate human language. There is a difference between the sexes: The males learn it better. It's more difficult to get them to learn this when they live in pairs, though this is better than having just one bird. Budgerigars are docile and appreciate human company. If you want them to climb onto your hand, you should respect certain rules. You should speak to them every day, so that they get used to your voice. Initially, you should place your hand in the cage carefully and quickly change the food and clean the cage, etc. At first, they'll flutter about scared, trying to escape. Little by little, they'll get used to these daily operations, to your presence, and to your voice. At this point, you can offer them a treat with your fingers, such as their favorite fruit. At first, they won't come close, but then they'll approach curiously and timidly until one day they'll dare to stretch out their neck, and take the food. After this, it won't take them very long to climb onto your hand. The member of the couple that hasn't done so yet will imitate the other one shortly afterward. The whole process can take from a few days to two months.

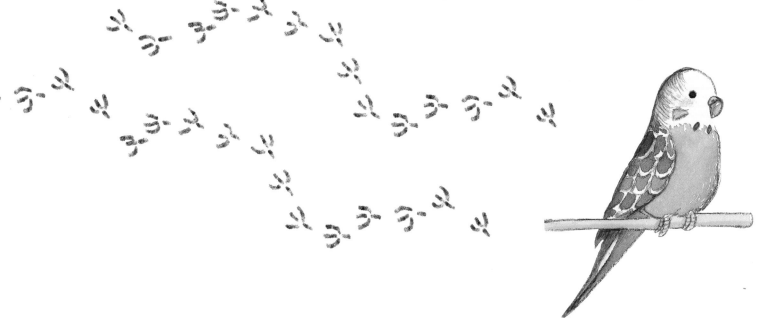

LET'S TAKE CARE OF OUR NEW BUDGERIGAR

English language version published
by Barron's Educational Series, Inc., 2008

Original title of the book in Catalan: *Un periquito en casa*
© Copyright GEMSER PUBLICATIONS S.L., 2008
Barcelona, Spain
Author: Alejandro Algarra
Translator: Sally-Ann Hopwood
Illustrator: Rosa Maria Curto

All inquiries should be addressed to:
Barron's Educational Series, Inc.
250 Wireless Boulevard
Hauppauge, New York 11788
www.barronseduc.com

ISBN-13: 978-0-7641-4066-2
ISBN-10: 0-7641-4066-3

Library of Congress Catalog Card. No. 2008926841

Printed in China
9 8 7 6 5 4 3 2 1